HEIRLOOM WOOD

HEIRLOOM
WOOD

A MODERN GUIDE TO CARVING SPOONS, BOWLS, BOARDS, AND OTHER HOMEWARES

MAX BAINBRIDGE

Photography: Dean Hearne
Design: Tina Smith

ABRAMS | NEW YORK

To my Nana, Jean Gray

Editor: Cristina Garces
Production Manager: Alex Cameron
Cover Design: John Gall

Library of Congress Control Number: 2016945895

ISBN: 978-1-4197-2476-3

Printed and bound in China
10 9 8 7 6 5 4 3 2 1

Abrams books are available at special discounts when purchased in quantity for premiums and promotions as well as fundraising or educational use. Special editions can also be created to specification. For details, contact specialsales@abramsbooks.com or the address below.

ABRAMS
The Art of Books

115 West 18th Street
New York, NY 10011
abramsbooks.com

FSC
www.fsc.org

MIX
Paper from
responsible sources
FSC® C016973

CONTENTS

INTRODUCTION

Wood has fascinated me for as long as I can remember. Everything from its smell and texture to its grain and color has always intrigued me, and I knew early on that it would be something I would work with. It is such a versatile and beautiful material that can be used in endless applications. One of my earliest childhood memories is firing a bow and arrow that I had made in our backyard. It had carved notches where the string sat at each end, and a handle carved into the bark revealing bright, white sapwood. I think it was this revelation that had such a lasting effect on me: the moment that I understood you could take a tree branch, and by the simple act of cutting, transform it into something useful—something that had a function. With a simple intervention, you can reveal qualities in the wood that at first glance are not visible. It is this infinite potential that

"Being a maker . . . is not just a job, it is a way of life."

leaves me feeling just as amazed and excited today as it did when I made that first cut all those years ago. I have been a "maker" all my life, but it is only in the past few years that I have started to work with wood as a craft. I made a conscious decision to hone my need to work with my hands into a set of skills. Being able to apply these skills to create objects that are not only beautiful in their form, but also functional and a pleasure to use, has become the driving force behind my work. Being a maker, woodworker, craftsman, carver, artist (whatever you want to call it), is not just a job, it is a way of life. Whenever I give an interview or talk to someone about what I do, I find myself coming back to the same way of phrasing it, and that is to say that "I live what I do." It is all-consuming. I am never not at work and I never have a day off. I think this is true of anyone who makes things or has a craft. I don't just do this as a means to an end—I do this period. There is never an end point, and that is what I find so exciting. My work is a process that is constantly evolving, constantly changing, and because of that I am constantly learning. I have approached writing this book in the same way that I would start to design a new shape of spoon or work with a new species of wood. It has been both daunting and exciting in equal measure. I have had to examine every aspect of my making process, break it down into separate steps, and then try to put them all back together on paper in a way that communicates my love of what I do. It has made me look at the way I use the tools I work with and how much I actually understand the nature of wood itself. It has made me scrutinize every aspect of my own methods and has taught me as much about my own craft as I wish to impart to my readers.

I hope that by writing this book I can excite other people about the craft of carving and the magic of making. It is important for me to pass on the skills I have learned so that others will get the same joy and satisfaction from the making process as I do. It is fundamental that people realize that

"Everything is designed to have a use, and everything that gets made is useful."

working with wood is something that everyone can do; you just need to have a starting point and a determination to learn. I started with a book, some YouTube videos, and a large box of band-aids. Three years later I am running my full-time business, Forest + Found, with my partner Abigail and making functional objects using traditional skills with contemporary design. In this book I will explore different techniques and processes including carving, filing, scorching, sanding, and waxing, all of which will be used to make objects that can be used in your home every day. If something doesn't have an actual function, then it doesn't usually leave the workshop. Everything is designed to have a use, and everything that gets made is useful.

Living in a city has an effect on everything I make: it determines where I work, the materials I use, and it influences aspects of my design process. Being based in Walthamstow in East London, I am surrounded by the

most diverse sources of both inspiration and materials. It is so important when living and working in a city to seek out the green spaces. It is these places that give you a change of environment and allow you time to breathe and think. I am fortunate to be in close proximity to Epping Forest, which covers 9 square miles of ancient woodland between the borders of North-East London and Essex. It's worth visiting your neighboring forests too, not only to stock up on a good selection of native hardwoods, but to retreat to the tranquillity of nature.

Being in an urban environment has meant I have had to seek out different sources of wood that can provide a sustainable and regular supply of material to work with. This does not mean just seeking out forests and green spaces. As well as working with forestry staff, I have also built up relationships with furniture- and cabinetmakers over the years. Getting to know other craftspeople can result in a regular supply of hardwood that would otherwise be burned or go to a landfill. Being able to take a by-

"You can get ahold of workable timber from just about anywhere."

product of someone else's industry and transform it into something useful is a very important part of how I work. I think it is vital to understand that you can get ahold of workable timber from just about anywhere. As long as you go through the proper channels and take the time to talk to people, most of the time they will be more than willing to help. Whether you live in a large city or a small town, all the information I have compiled in this book is just as valid and useful. It will enable you to discover what is available to you and where to go to find it.

One of the most important things to me is that I enjoy what I do. Sometimes carving can be really hard work. You might get to a stage in a project that proves particularly difficult or stubborn and it is then that I like to take five minutes to have a breather and more often than not make a cup of coffee. It is far more productive to step back and think of a solution rather than continue and get frustrated. I have learned the hard way that by plowing ahead you can end up making silly mistakes or worse, injuring yourself. Health and safety is something I take very seriously and with a few simple checks and precautions it is something that doesn't need to get in the way or take up much time. The main things to think about are yourself, your surroundings, your materials, and your tools. Give yourself time before starting a new project to take note of what you are going to make, what tools and materials you will need, where you are going to be working, and most importantly, that you feel up to the challenge. Trying to work if you are stressed, tired, or your mind is not focused can be dangerous to yourself as well as others around you. The projects in this book are designed to build on your skill levels at each stage, so you should feel confident and excited about taking on each new challenge. Carving is at its most enjoyable when you are not constrained by a deadline. I want to encourage people to understand that craft takes time and is always the better for it.

"Understand that craft takes time and is always the better for it."

My practice has always been involved in contemporary design, but underpinning this is the constant narrative of traditional craft. I hope that people can use this book as a springboard to learning a new way of working that allows them to go on to design and make their own things. I want to emphasize that as well as making spoons, woodcarving can benefit you in a lot of ways. It can improve your state of mind by letting you step out of modern fast-paced living and slowing things down. As you concentrate on achieving the perfect cut on the edge of a board or sweep of a handle, you begin to understand the subtleties that wood affords. Wherever you are in the world, carving allows the simple pleasure of being in touch with the outdoors and learning how to make use of our natural resources. I hope that by the end of this book you will have the knowledge and excitement to carry on exploring this craft that I have fallen in love with.

SOURCING WOOD

Knowing where to get your materials can make all the difference when starting to learn how to carve. Finding a reliable source of timber at a relatively low cost will allow you to experiment and play without worrying about how much your materials have cost you. There are four main sources I get my wood from, all of which do not cost very much and sometimes can even be free.

The Local Forest Service

I am fortunate enough to be a short drive away from Epping Forest, which is run by the City of London Corporation. I did a bit of research and was able to get in contact with one of the employees from the Forestry Commission. He was more than happy to show me what species of trees they manage and let me hunt through the huge piles of wood they amass as part of the regular management of the forest.

I work a lot with birch as it is a fast growing species where I live and is constantly being thinned out to maintain a healthy balance within the forest. Your local forest service may be able to point you in the direction of similar native hardwoods. Exactly which wood is available depends on whether a tree needs storm-damaged limbs to be removed or if one gets rot and needs to be taken down safely. However, I find that sourcing wood this way is a great way to work as you are constantly surprised and challenged by what is available. It makes you flexible with your designs and shapes, as you cannot rely on getting a specific type of wood time and time again. It is this variety that I find so exciting and you will find the same diversity and availability of species working with any local forest service that you come across.

Having made contact with the Forestry Commission, I now arrange meetings with one of the forestry workers at their base, and we go out to a site within the forest where they have been working so I can see what is available. They are happy for me to sift through and pick and choose until I have a car full of wood. The arrangement I have is to make a small donation to the Forestry Commission as a token of appreciation and spread the word about the great work they are doing. You will find every forest service will want to work differently, but if you take the time to explain who you are and what it is you want the wood for, people are usually more than willing to help. It is all about going through the right channels and being respectful of people and their time. I am more than happy to work around the schedules of the people who work at the commission because it means I can get a fantastic source of sustainable, native hardwoods. It also means I get to spend a morning in a beautiful green space and build up working relationships with local authorities.

Tree Surgeons

The ability to tune in to the sound of a chainsaw nearby can be a very worthwhile skill. On several occasions I have dropped whatever I was doing at the time and dashed out to track down the sound of a chainsaw. Tree surgeons operate all over, from small towns to big cities. If you see tree surgeons at work, it is always worth asking them what they are working on and if they would be willing to let you take a few bits of what they are cutting down. It is important to always make sure you wait until it is safe to approach them, for their and your own safety. When the saw stops and you can see them moving wood to their truck, it is usually a good time to go and speak to them.

Tree surgeons can be a fantastic source of native hardwoods as well as a way of getting ahold of some more varied and exotic varieties of wood. A lot of the time the smaller branches go straight through the chipper first, so if you can keep them from shredding everything all at once you can usually get yourself some good-sized pieces that are still workable.

Other Makers

Building up relationships with other makers and craftsmen can be a fantastic source of material. Not only is it important to be part of a creative community, but I have also found that other people's waste materials can sometimes be perfect for what you need. I work with several carpenters and cabinetmakers who produce large amounts of offcuts that they have no use for. More often than not they have to pay to get rid of excess wood, so it helps them if you are able to take this unwanted material off their hands. If you take the time to talk to people and explain what it is you do and what you are looking for, then through these conversations, mutual working relationships are born.

Lumber Suppliers

Some lumber suppliers, usually the ones that specialize in hardwoods, will keep a good selection of offcuts. One close to me has an onsite sawmill where they can cut, plane, and rip wood to size for their customers, which inevitably produces offcuts in varying shapes and sizes, some of which are just the right size and thickness for my projects.

It is always worth going to rummage around a lumber yard if they have a place where they keep their offcuts, as you can stumble across some really interesting species of wood and, because of the small sizes, they are usually willing to let you have them for a very reasonable price. Bear in mind that not every lumber supplier specializes in native hardwoods, so it is worth doing some research and finding one that you like before you visit.

CHOOSING WOOD

Choosing the correct type of wood for your project is crucial. Getting to know the difference between hardwoods and softwoods will allow you to pick the right species and type of wood to work with. Throughout this book I will be using a variety of different hardwoods. Softwoods are not really suitable for carving. They have a widely spaced grain and their soft surface makes them prone to tearing. Softwood can also be quite porous so is not suitable for making utensils and bowls that will come into contact with food or liquid. Hardwoods, on the other hand, tend to be close-grained and very strong, ideal for making objects that are used daily.

In my day-to-day practice, I work with a selection of green hardwood, reclaimed hardwood, and hardwood offcuts. The term "green wood" refers to wood that has been freshly cut, and still holds a lot of moisture, unlike seasoned wood, which has been left to dry over time. Both green wood and seasoned wood have their advantages and disadvantages when carving. Green wood is far easier to work with as the high moisture content makes the fibers of the wood softer and more flexible. This allows the blade of your knife to cut through the fibers with greater ease. However, unlike seasoned wood, it can crack and warp as it dries. Seasoned wood is much tougher to carve, as the fibers, being dry, are very hard and rigid. You will find that your knives need to be sharpened more frequently when working with seasoned wood, but you will be able to rely on its stability as

> *"Getting to know the difference between hardwoods and softwoods will allow you to pick the right species."*

what species it is. It is always worth doing some research online to identify the species, which is best done by looking at the bark and shape of the leaves, and secondly to make sure that what you have gathered and found is not poisonous. If you are getting it from a lumber supplier, forest service, or tree surgeon then you can ask them what kind of wood it is. But there are some great websites you can use to check these characteristics if you are not sure: www.wood-database.com is my go-to site to

"Adapt designs and work with the character of the material."

all cracks and warps have already happened during the drying process. I wanted to use both green and seasoned wood in this book to show that if you know how to approach working with them, and understand that a green piece of birch will behave differently than a seasoned piece of birch, it is well worth working with both. It offers you twice as much scope for getting your hands on usable timber and gives you insight into which kinds of wood are best suited for the project you have in your head. You will find that if you are sourcing wood from tree surgeons or forest services, it will most likely be freshly cut and green. If you have managed to get ahold of hardwood offcuts or scraps from a lumber supplier, the likelihood is that these have been kiln-dried and well seasoned. You can season green wood yourself, which means storing it in a well ventilated dry space, such as a garden shed, and leaving it for prolonged periods of time. It can sometimes take up to two years for wood to completely dry out, though.

You also have to think about what kind of wood you are sourcing, especially if you are not sure

identify a species and check for toxicity. It takes only a few minutes of research to give you peace of mind that you can use your wood safely.

Storing wood is also something you need to think about. Seasoned hardwood and offcuts can be stored easily enough without really having to do anything. They just need to be in dry conditions and not in direct contact with a heat source. Green wood, however, requires a little bit more attention. If you are going to be working with it right away, then you don't need to worry about storing it, but if you want to be able to store wood to work over time, then you need to take a few simple steps. There are lots of different ways people store green

cracks if they appear. Some of my favorite objects I have made have been the result of using timber that developed cracks as I was working with it. It teaches you how to adapt designs and work with the character of the material.

I have tried to use a different species of hardwood for each project in the book to demonstrate the wide variety of timber that is readily available. You can, of course, make all of the projects in this book from one type of wood. I have used green oak for the Small Bowl on page 98

"Wood is a natural material and there is always going to be a level of unpredictability to it."

wood. The main goals are to prevent it from drying out too quickly and splitting. You can buy all sorts of wax sealants and compounds, which work well but can be quite expensive. I have seen people put green wood in the freezer and even in large barrels of water covered in candle wax. I think it is worth experimenting to see what works best for you, but I always recommend simplicity. I tend to use PVA glue on the end of thinner branches and lengths of green wood to seal the moisture in. If I am cutting up some larger logs, then I prefer to split them in half and wrap them in plastic wrap or plastic bags and keep them in a cool, dark place. It is important to split any logs in half as, if left whole, any evaporating moisture will cause the wood to shrink, which builds up tension and results in cracks and splits opening up. If left, the cracks can travel the full length of the log inside, making your life difficult when trying to find a solid piece to work with. There is, however, only so much you can do. Wood is a natural material and there is always going to be a level of unpredictability to it. Sometimes you just have to go with it and work with the splits and

for example, but there is no reason you couldn't use birch or chestnut instead. I think it is nice to work with what is available locally to you and especially if you are just starting out, it is great to be able to source wood close by. In each project I give a brief explanation of why I have chosen to work with each different wood. You can choose to follow my example, but in no way is it a rule to stick by. I always choose wood for its practicality, but often when there are several suitable kinds of wood, I then make a choice based on aesthetics and how I want an object to look.

WOOD TYPES

1. Oak (Green)

When green, oak can be easily worked with hand tools, making it a very good choice for bowls and vessels.

2. Birch

Birch can be used for a wide range of items. Its uniform grain and texture make it a very reliable carving material. It has the ability to be both strong and lightweight at the same time.

3. Reclaimed Oak

Oak is incredibly strong and robust. It's perfect for items that will see a lot of day-to-day use. When seasoned, it can be quite tough to work with, but the finished item will last.

4. Chestnut

Chestnut is both strong and flexible. It has a beautiful grain and texture, and so is ideal for items that will be used on a daily basis.

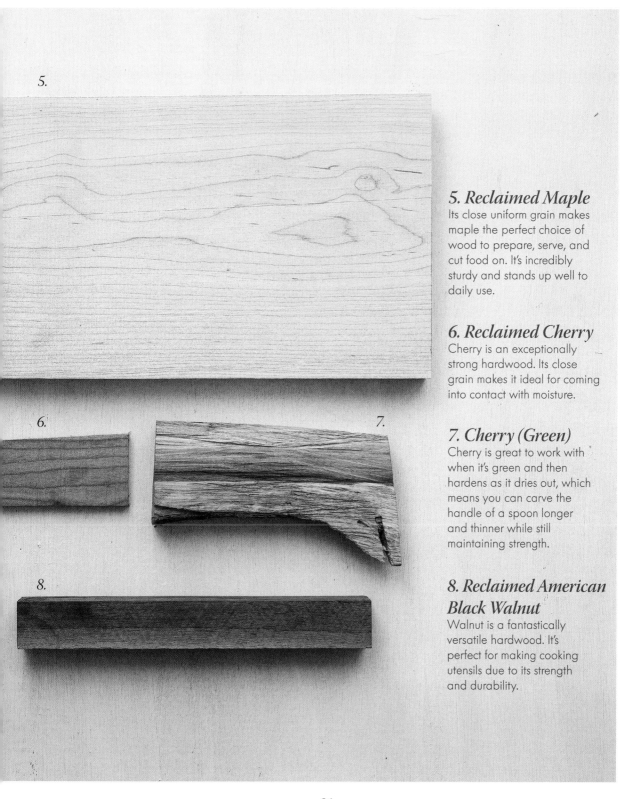

5.

5. Reclaimed Maple
Its close uniform grain makes maple the perfect choice of wood to prepare, serve, and cut food on. It's incredibly sturdy and stands up well to daily use.

6. Reclaimed Cherry
Cherry is an exceptionally strong hardwood. Its close grain makes it ideal for coming into contact with moisture.

7. Cherry (Green)
Cherry is great to work with when it's green and then hardens as it dries out, which means you can carve the handle of a spoon longer and thinner while still maintaining strength.

8. Reclaimed American Black Walnut
Walnut is a fantastically versatile hardwood. It's perfect for making cooking utensils due to its strength and durability.

6.

7.

8.

TOOLS

Having the right tools for the job is essential. The tools I use in this book are relatively inexpensive and easy to find. You don't need a huge arsenal of tools and equipment to be able to carve and make. The two main tools I use throughout this book are the hook knife and the straight knife. There are a lot of variations on the ones I will be using, but these two are tried and tested. Not only do they perform really well, they are also inexpensive and you can find them just about anywhere. For further information on sources, see page 138.

The hook knife, with its distinctive curved blade, is designed for hollowing or scooping out a concave form, which is why it is so perfectly suited to carving the bowls of spoons. The straight knife performs many different tasks from removing bulk waste to the fine detail of finishing cuts. You will find both of these knives in any woodcarver's toolbox, and they are great places to start when setting out. They will quickly become your essential tools from which you can build up a collection of more varied and specialized tools, if you wish to do so.

Tools in their own right are exceptionally pleasing objects. In Scandinavia there is a strong tradition of decorating carving tools with ornately carved handles, patterned leather sheaths, and painstakingly sculpted guards made from horn and antler. The same level of care and respect that goes into looking after and making the tools reflects the care that then goes into using them. It is this lesson that I try to remember when using my tools, as the best craftsmanship begins with understanding how your tools behave and work. I often find if I

am in the workshop talking to someone, I will look down and find myself carving a spoon I have picked up absentmindedly. Using my tools has become second nature to me. You start to get a feel for them, and as you do you begin to understand their weight and the way they fit in your hand. When you are comfortable with the tools you are using they almost become an extension of your hands, allowing you to work confidently.

"Tools in their own right are exceptionally pleasing objects."

As you begin to take on new challenges and projects, you will naturally find which tools are best suited for a specific job. You may find yourself working with every tool you have to create that one perfect spoon, or you may prefer to stick with one or two knives. There is no right or wrong way of reaching that end goal. Whatever works for you the best will allow you to produce the best work. This book is about encouraging you to try and to explore carving in a way that suits you. Each of us will find our hands like to work in different ways.

1.

2.

3.

1. G Clamp

The G clamp is a really useful piece of equipment if you are working with chisels or using the reverse scoop cut with the crook knife. It allows you to secure the workpiece to a desk or workbench freeing up both hands to grip and control your tools.

2. Drill

Being able to make clean holes quickly and efficiently using a drill can make a big difference to a project. You do not need anything expensive or state of the art; as long as it works and you can use it safely, then it is fit for its purpose.

3. Jigsaw

I use a jigsaw for a lot of the projects in this book. It gives you the opportunity to make controlled cuts and minimize wastage as well as speed up the process. As with the drill, you don't need to spend vast amounts of money on something that is laser guided and has lots of different features. As long as it has the power to cut through hardwood, it will be fine. I most often use a curve cut blade for my projects.

4. Carving Gouges

These gouges are a great addition to your tool arsenal. They offer you a different way of carving, and come in all different shapes and sizes. The two I will be using are relatively small and good for finer, more detailed work.

4.

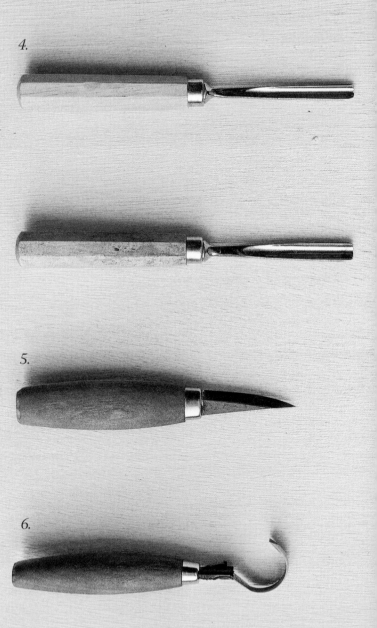

5.

6.

7.

8.

5. *Mora 120 Straight Knife*

This is a classic woodcarving knife, and you will find yourself using it more than any other tool for the projects in this book. With over a century of skill and passion behind the Mora brand, these Swedish knives have always been a go-to tool for craftsmen. The craftsmanship that goes into making each knife is tried and tested and is evident as soon as you start using one.

6. *Mora 162 Hook Knife*

This curved double-edged blade allows you to make a variety of rounded cuts. By using different sections of the blade, you can achieve delicate refinement as well as deep, hollowing cuts. It is an extremely versatile tool.

7. *Shinto Saw Rasp*

This is quite a specialty tool but still very affordable. It allows you to shape and sculpt the surfaces of wood and remove waste material quickly and efficiently. It has a coarse and a fine side, which means you can really refine the shapes you are creating.

8. *Ax*

The ax is a fantastically versatile tool, especially if you are working with greenwood. If I am not in my workshop, I can take an ax and two carving knives out, allowing me to work just about anywhere. The ax pictured is a hatchet, which due to its small size makes it perfect for processing smaller pieces of wood into spoon blanks.

KNIFE GRIPS

Knife grips are one of the most important elements of technique that I cover in this book. As you work your way through the projects, I encourage you to revisit this chapter as you improve your understanding of how to use your knives while working. Here is a selection of different grips and cuts that will allow you to cut and shape wood efficiently and safely. Half the battle is making sure you are aware of where your fingers are positioned in relation to the blade and not to take any unnecessary risks. It doesn't take long to make sure you are safe when working. My advice is to take a piece of scrap wood and practice these techniques. It is always better to master the basics on waste material before starting out on a specific project.

▼ *Straight Knife: Push Cut*

Hold the knife in your dominant hand, and use your other hand to support the workpiece. Bring your thumb from the workpiece to the top of the handle where it meets the blade. Push away from the body, which will allow you to apply the exact amount of pressure required for the cut, while using your dominant hand to grip the knife and control the direction of the blade. This cut can be performed either standing or sitting. Either way you will find it most comfortable and have maximum control if you work close to your body. If you imagine you have the arms of a T. rex it will give you an idea of the position your hands should be in relation to your chest. You will use this cut the most frequently when working, so it is a good idea to familiarize yourself with it early on.

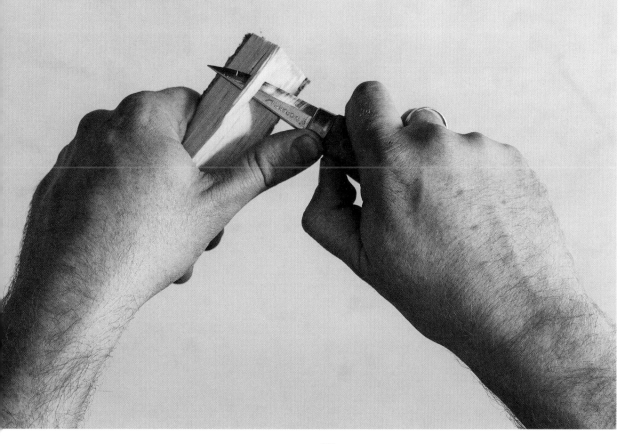

▼ Straight Knife: Detail Cut

This cut is useful for when you are getting down to the finer details of a project and for shaping and texturing the surface. Using the knife in your dominant hand and holding the workpiece in your other, bring the thumb of the supporting hand to the back of the blade. This position will change depending on the size of the workpiece and the depth of cut required. For example, on a small piece your thumb might be near the tip of the blade giving you maximum control. Using a similar motion to the push cut, apply pressure with your thumb and guide the blade with your dominant hand.

▶ Straight Knife: Pull Cut

Support one end of the workpiece in your hand, and the other on your chest (wearing an apron or protective shirt is recommended). Start the cut in front of your supporting hand. Applying even pressure and keeping the blade quite flat to the surface of the wood, draw the blade toward yourself. You are not looking for a quick, powerful motion here. You are aiming for maximum control with a clear view to where the blade is going to stop. This is a very useful technique that allows you to work longer lengths of wood while delivering controlled and even straight cuts. This way of working requires you to cut toward yourself, which may seem counterintuitive and go against everything you have ever been told when using a knife, but if done safely it is like any other carving technique. Keeping your hands and fingers behind the blade is crucial for this type of cut.

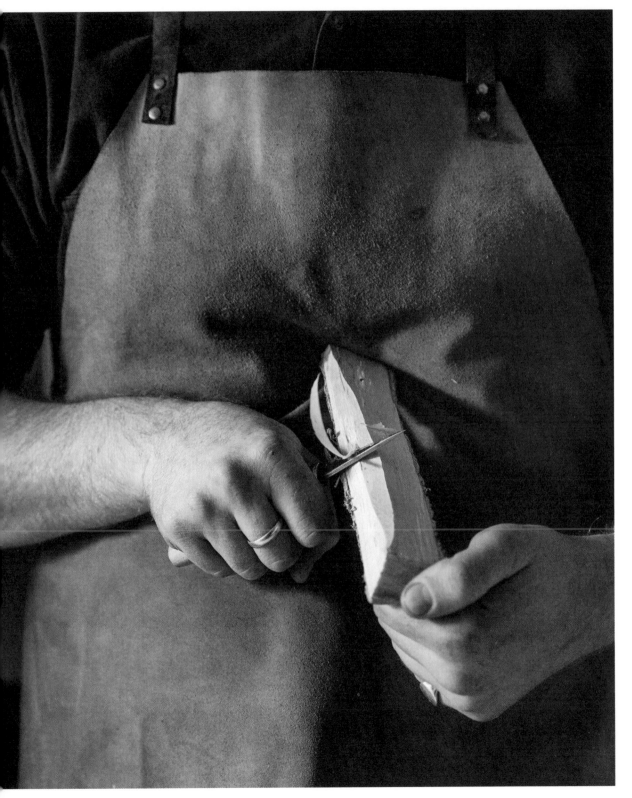

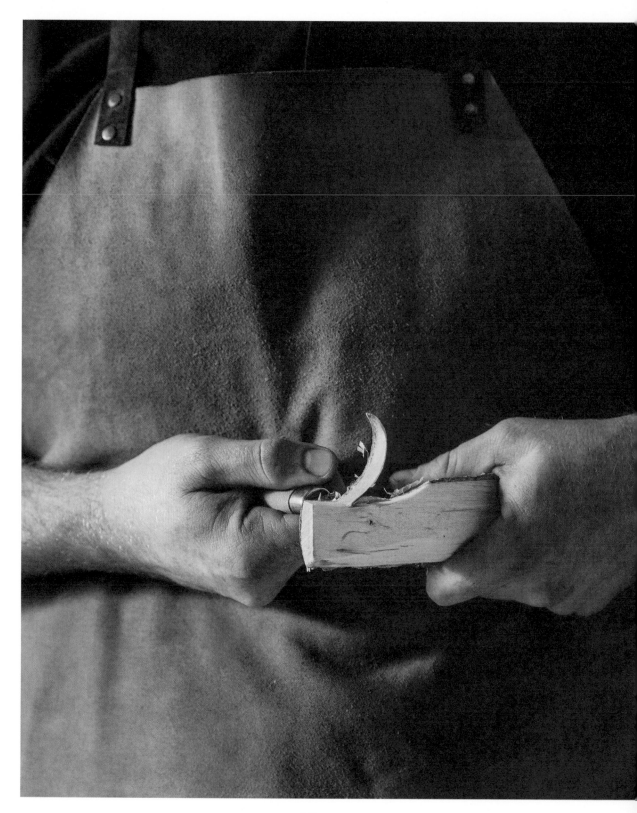

◀ *Straight Knife: Scissor Cut*

This, as the name suggests, involves the blade and the workpiece crossing each other in a similar way to the action of a pair of scissors. Working close to your body, keeping your elbows tucked in (remember the T. rex), hold the knife in your dominant hand and the workpiece in your other. Present the blade to the surface of the wood and, using your arms to power the cut, tuck both elbows into your ribs and allow your hands to be drawn apart, thus making the cut. This is a very useful way of removing both large amounts of stock material and for finer more detailed cuts. It is also a very safe way of working, as the hand that is holding the knife can't travel past a certain point away from your body as it is restricted by the position of your arms.

▼ *Hook Knife: Scoop Cut*

Hold the hook knife in your dominant hand with the tip of the blade facing straight up. Supporting the workpiece in your other hand, present the bevel of the blade to the surface of the wood. Using the thumb of your dominant hand as a support at the back of the workpiece, roll your hand back away from yourself while making the cut toward yourself. During this cut your thumb should act as an anchor point; make sure it stays below the edge of the workpiece and out of the way of the blade.

▼ Hook Knife: Push Cut

Hold the knife in your dominant hand and the workpiece in your other. Present the blade to the surface of the wood. Using the thumb of the hand that is gripping the workpiece, apply pressure away from yourself to make the cut. This is an effective way of getting more power into the cut, allowing you to remove stock material efficiently.

▶ Hook Knife: Reverse Scoop Cut

Hold the knife in your dominant hand with the blade facing down. Make contact with the surface of the workpiece. Use the bevel of the knife to roll through the cut away from yourself, making an upward motion with your wrist as you push through the cut. The hand holding the workpiece will act as an anchor. This cut is best done on a work surface for maximum stability.

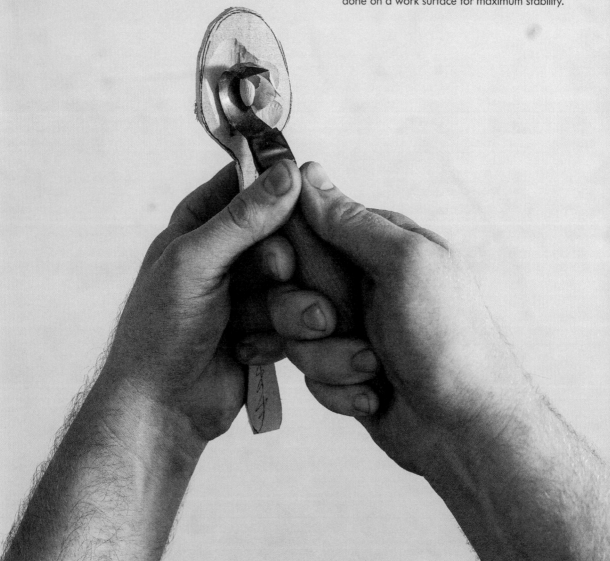

▼ Ax: Splitting Wood

Hand positioning is really important when using your ax. Here the ax is being used to split a section of branch in half. Rather than striking down with the ax onto the wood, it is placed carefully with the blade centered on the surface and then the ax is struck with a mallet—this is a far safer and more precise way to split wood. Make sure you keep a firm grip on the bottom third of the handle, keeping your arm straight and your hand away from the head of the ax.

▼ *Ax: Cutting*

When using the ax to rough out the shape of your spoon, keep your hand and fingers holding the work piece well out of the way, tucking your thumb under your fingers away from the surface you are working on. You should be looking to grip between the middle and top section of the handle, which will give you maximum control and prevent you from making bigger swings that are less easy to control. You will find the closer to the head of the ax you grip the handle, the smaller your cuts will become, and this allows you to make finer cuts on the workpiece.

EATING SPOON

Create an eating spoon from birch

Rough dimensions: 1½ × ⅜ × 7⅞ in (4 × 1 × 20cm)

The eating spoon is something that has been made throughout history in many different shapes and sizes. It is one of the most utilitarian of spoons I make and probably gets the most use, but it remains one of the most elegant in its simplicity and form. The shape has evolved with every one I have made, tweaking the size of the bowl or altering the length of the handle. All these adjustments have resulted in a spoon that has the right proportions and balance to make a utensil that is a joy to eat with. The aim is to create a spoon that resonates with you and becomes something that you look forward to using every day.

Tools:
ax
mallet (a section of branch will also work well)
pencil
template (paper/cardstock)
hook knife
straight knife
sandpaper (see page 118)
cloth
beeswax salve (see page 122)

Wood:
green birch

Selecting the right piece of wood is a really important part of the process. For this project I use birch. It's a fantastically versatile species of wood and a great starting point for carving. Select a section of branch that has as few knots as possible so that you have enough workable and uninterrupted wood once the log has been split.

1 Place the birch log on a stable cutting block (a large round log serves well as a chopping block). Place the ax in line with the middle of the end of the piece of timber. Using the mallet, strike down, making sure to hit the back of the ax head and not the handle.

2 Once you have two halves of the log, choose the one with the flatter face. Create a template with thick paper or cardstock, using the dimensions on page 47 and the photos on page 46 and 51 as a guide, and cut it out. Use it to mark out your design in the center of the piece of wood. Start to cut away with the ax to rough out the spoon blank, removing the stock material. Always work cutting from the middle of the log down to your cutting block, making sure your ax never comes near your hands. You can keep moving and turning the blank as you shape.

3 Once you have your spoon roughed out, the next step is to carve the bowl. Using the hook knife and scoop cut, work across the grain from the far side of the bowl toward yourself. You won't need to apply a lot of pressure with the knife—since the wood is green, it gives very little resistance to the blade, which makes it very easy to work.

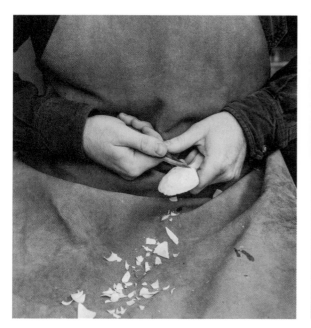

4 Now that you have hollowed out the bowl of the spoon, you can start to shape and refine the back of the spoon with the straight knife, using the push cut. Make sure to work in one direction from the middle of the back of the spoon up, and then change direction working from the middle down to the shoulders. This should stop you cutting against the grain and experiencing unnecessary resistance.

5 After you have shaped the back of the spoon, you can work on refining the handle and the transition of the shoulders with the straight knife by using a combination of the pull cut and push cut. Once your general shape emerges, you can start using the detail cut to refine areas of your design.

6 Now that you have refined the shape and are happy with the balance and form of the spoon, you can start to sand. The one rule to remember here is always to sand with the grain; this will ensure that you achieve a silky smooth finish and avoid creating scratches, which are then difficult to get out. Work your way up through the grits, starting at 120-grit moving through to 320-grit, until you are happy with the surface finish.

7 Apply a generous coat of the beeswax salve with a clean cloth and allow it to soak in overnight. The following morning you can give the spoon a good rub all over to work in any remaining salve and polish the surface.

② SPATULA

Use cherry offcuts to create a spatula

Rough dimensions: 2 × ¼ × 14½ in (5 × 0.5 × 36cm)

The design for this spatula came about from an offcut of a cooking spoon. I had trimmed the back down and was about to throw the leftover scrap into the wood burner when I realized there was scope to develop the shape, and with a bit of playing around, this simple but elegant spatula was formed. The beauty of this design is that it only requires a really thin piece of wood, allowing you to use even the most unremarkable pieces of offcuts. It is also a good utensil on which to practice honing your skills using the straight knife. If you happen to have a piece of wood that is close to the final shape, then you may not need to use a jigsaw to cut out the template—just use the straight knife to remove the waste material.

Tools:
pencil
template (paper/cardstock)
jigsaw with curve cut blade
clamp
straight knife
sandpaper (see page 118)
cloth
beeswax salve (see page 122)

Wood:
cherry

The piece of cherry I use in this project came from a local lumber supplier, which is the best place to look if you want a small, inexpensive piece of wood. Cherry is a strong hardwood, which is perfect for making utensils that have long handles and will be used for stirring. It is important to choose a wood that will stand up to its end use.

1 Create a template with thick paper or cardstock, using the dimensions above and the photo at left as a guide. Use it to mark out the shape of your spatula. It is a good idea to think carefully about the handle length, as this will have an impact on how easy it is to use. You can always take wood away, but you cannot put it back, so I advise keeping the handle a little longer than required when cutting it out. You can always shorten it later.

 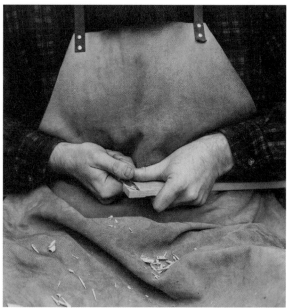

2 Cut out the spatula blank using a jigsaw with a curve cut blade. You can purchase a curve cut blade from your local DIY store. The reason I stipulate this specific blade is that it makes cutting curved shapes far more accurate and safe.

3 Work on shaping the head of the spatula first with the straight knife. Use the scissor cut method to remove waste from the flat face of your spatula on both sides until you have a thickness you are happy with.

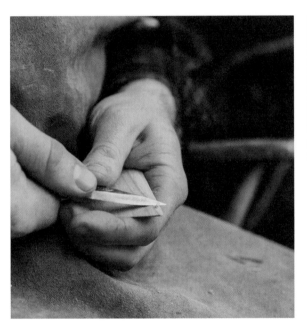

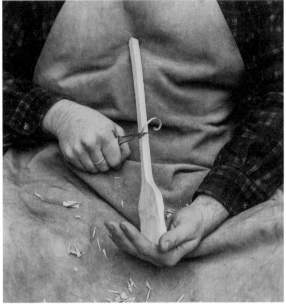

4 Now use the detail cut to refine the shape and carefully cut the bevel on the edge of the spatula head. This is crucial for the spatula's end function, as this bevel allows you to cook and stir with ease.

5 The pull cut works well to remove long lengths of waste as you fashion the handle. With the head of the spatula held in your hand, and the handle resting on your chest, work the cuts toward your body to begin shaping the handle. To maintain smooth cuts, you will need to turn the workpiece so that you are holding the end of the handle with the head against your chest. This change of direction in cuts keeps you from cutting through the grain and gives you a smooth, even finish.

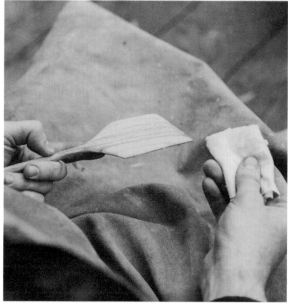

6 Once you are happy with the shape and balance of the spatula, you can move on to sanding. It is really important to get a fine, crisp finish on the bevel, giving you a utensil that is easy to use as well as being beautifully formed. To maintain the definition of the bevel, avoid rounding the end off too much when sanding.

7 Give the spatula a rub down to remove any sawdust. Apply a thick coat of beeswax salve and allow it to soak in overnight. Buff any excess off the next morning to give a clean finish.

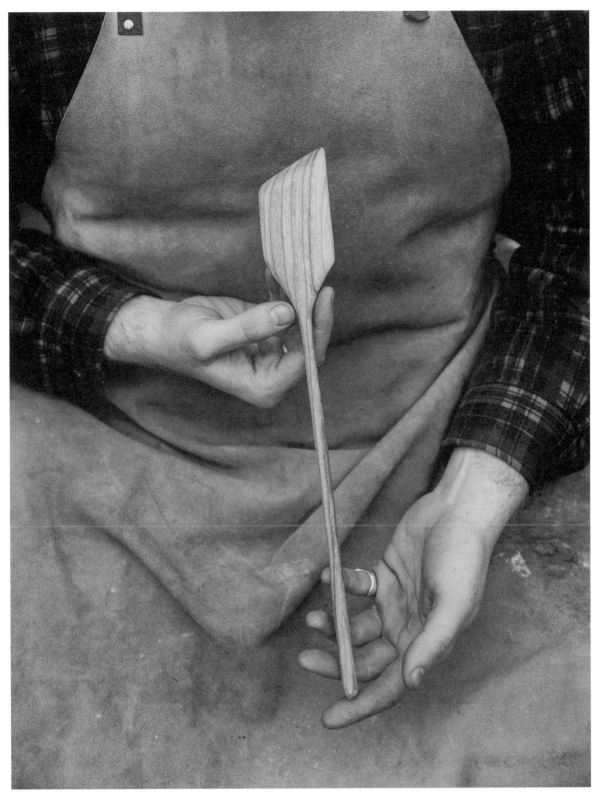

3

COOKING SPOON

Make a cooking spoon using reclaimed walnut

Rough dimensions: 2⅜ × ⅜ × 14½ in (6 × 1 × 36cm)

A cooking spoon is something everyone has in their kitchen and uses on a daily basis. When I designed this spoon I wanted to make something that has a delicate aesthetic but is in fact incredibly strong and, most importantly, usable. Carving this cooking spoon will build on the techniques you used when making the spatula. Similar principles will apply to working the handle, and you will be able to practice refining a much larger bowl of a spoon. You may not need to use a jigsaw if the shape of the piece of wood you are starting with is a similar size and shape to your end design—just draw out your template and start carving with a straight knife.

Tools:
pencil
template (paper/cardstock)
jigsaw with curve cut blade
clamp
hook knife
straight knife
sandpaper (see page 118)
cloth
beeswax salve (see page 122)

Wood:
walnut

All the walnut I work with comes from a local cabinetmaker. He has plenty of offcuts that are too small for him to use but are perfect for making spoons from. Walnut is a great choice of wood for making cooking spoons, as it is strong, flexible, and handles moisture well.

1 Create a template with thick paper or cardstock, using the dimensions above and the photo at left as a guide. Use it to mark out your shape on your piece of walnut. To minimize waste, angle the handle to one side, which means you should be able to get two spoons from the same piece of wood. When marking out, try to avoid any knots or cracks in the wood as these can weaken the handle or create a hole in the bowl of the spoon.

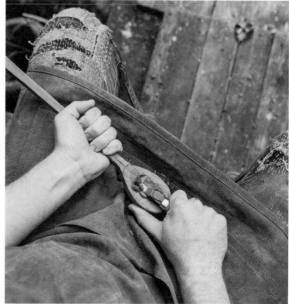

2 Secure your workpiece to a bench and cut out using a jigsaw with a curve cut blade. Leave around a millimeter of material around the template line. This will allow you to work right up to the perimeter when carving without worrying about cutting through the edge of the bowl.

3 Start to carve out the bowl of the spoon with the hook knife, working from the furthest side of the bowl toward yourself using the scoop cut. You will need to move the spoon around in your supporting hand without altering the cutting grip to ensure you get an even cut distribution.

 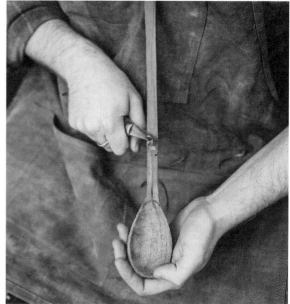

4 You can also use the push cut with the hook knife, which allows you to shape the rim more accurately and get a regular depth across the bowl of the spoon.

5 Once the bowl of the spoon has reached the depth you are happy with, you can start to shape the handle using the straight knife and the pull cut as you did for the spatula.

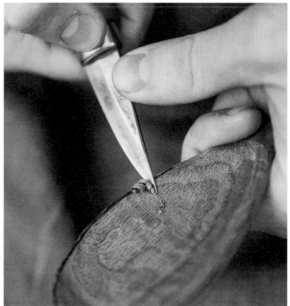

6 Now you can start to refine the shape of the back of the bowl and the shoulders with the straight knife, using a combination of both the push cut and detail cut. Keep removing waste material until you are happy with the thickness of the bowl and the join of the shoulders.

7 It is a good idea to take some time with the detail cut to even out the rim of the spoon, making sure you achieve a consistent thickness all the way around. This will make sanding a lot easier since you won't need to remove waste material through sanding.

8 Sand the spoon, working with the grain of the wood. You will find that the bowl of the spoon needs more sanding to even out the surface. I find manipulating the sandpaper and wrapping a section around your thumb or finger works well, as this allows you more control and gives you a feel for the surface texture as you are sanding.

9 Walnut dust is extremely fine, so make sure to give the spoon a thorough rub down with a cloth before applying a good layer of beeswax salve. Let it soak in overnight, then rub down with a clean cloth the following day.

4

BUTTER KNIFE

Carve a butter knife from cherry

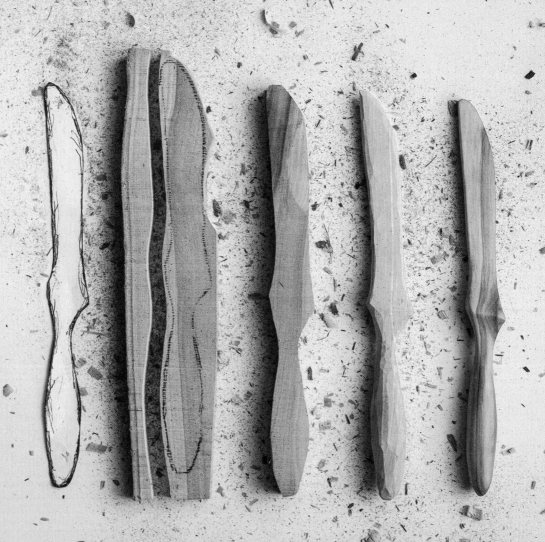

Rough dimensions: ¾ × ⅜ × 8¼ in (2 × 1 × 21cm)

The butter knife is the perfect project for refining your knife work. You will be using one knife in this project, showing you that with the right application you can achieve a varied range of shapes and finishes with a single tool. The butter knife is a tricky utensil to make due to it being small with a detailed shape. However, you will learn to control small detailed cuts and experiment with the shape that feels most comfortable in your own hand. If you have drawn out your shape and there is not a lot of waste material around your design, then you may not need to use the jigsaw—just use the straight knife to remove the waste wood.

Tools:
pencil
template (paper/cardstock)
jigsaw with curve cut blade
clamp
straight knife
sandpaper (see page 118)
cloth
beeswax salve (see page 118)

Wood:
cherry

Cherry is a perfect choice of wood for a butter knife because it has a close grain and is very hard when dry so will stand up to daily use very well. Another reason I choose to make butter knives from cherry is to display the amazing colors that run through the heartwood. With the right selection of timber you can make a utensil that has beautiful figuring, showing off the wood to its best advantage.

1 Create a template with thick paper or cardstock, using the dimensions above and the photo at left as a guide. Start by choosing the section you want to make your butter knife from. With cherry, the heartwood has fantastic variations in color, so deciding where to position and draw out your template is key.

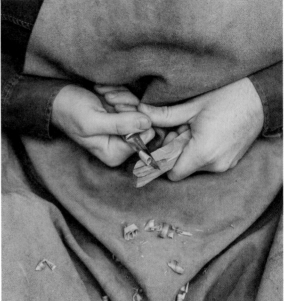

2 Secure the workpiece to the workbench and, using a jigsaw, cut out the butter knife blank, making sure to use a curve cut blade to cut around the narrow shape accurately.

3 Start by working the blade section of the butter knife with the straight knife. Using the scissor cut, start thinning out the shape by keeping the blade of your cutting knife flat to the surface. This will allow you to remove thin slivers of waste material.

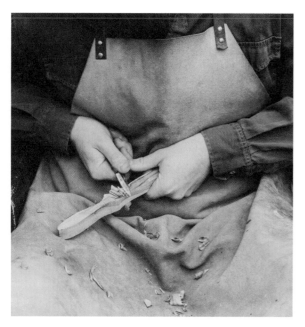

4 Now start working on the join between the blade and the shoulders of the butter knife as it transitions into the handle. Use the push cut to create short curls as you start to define the curves of the shoulders.

5 When you have removed enough waste material you can start refining the shape of the handle using the detail cut. To do this, work slowly from the shoulders down to the end of the handle, concentrating on producing a comfortable shape that sits well in the hand.

6 Before starting to sand the butter knife, think about the grain direction. Since the curves of the handle meet the blade, it can be slightly awkward to sand with the grain, but it is important that you try to achieve this to get a clean finish. To do so, move the workpiece around in your hands to find the angle that works best. Work up through the grits of sandpaper starting at 120-grit moving through to 320-grit.

7 Give the butter knife a wipe down with a cloth to remove any sawdust and apply a generous coat of the beeswax salve. Let soak overnight and then buff off with a clean cloth the next morning.

5

COFFEE SCOOP

Use chestnut to carve a coffee scoop

Rough dimensions: 2½ × 1 × 5⅛ in (6.5 × 2.5 × 13cm)

This is possibly one of my favorite designs to make. It uses a lot of different techniques and can be quite challenging since you are working on something that is relatively small. There are many different elements that require strength and concentration to achieve. The techniques you will learn making this scoop will allow you to make any number of other designs and shapes of scoop or spoon with a deep bowl. Although I use and make these scoops for coffee, they can equally be used for any other dry goods.

Tools:
pencil
template (paper/cardstock)
jigsaw with curve cut blade
clamp
hook knife
straight knife
sandpaper (see page 118)
cloth
beeswax salve (see page 122)

Wood:
chestnut

Chestnut is sometimes referred to as "poor man's oak" but I think it is a great native hardwood. It is incredibly versatile and its color can vary hugely, giving you tones of lightest tan right through to a deep chocolate brown. Its grain can run true and straight and then surprise you with fantastic swirls and patterns, which is something to take into consideration when working with it, as these can make it trickier to carve.

1 Selecting the right piece of wood is especially important for this project. Choose a section where the grain is running nice and straight and make sure you check the wood all the way around for any signs of knots or cracks. The bowl on the coffee scoop is quite deep and you need to make sure there are no defects running through it. Once you have selected a section, create a template with thick paper or cardstock, using the dimensions above and the photos at left and on page 83 as a guide. Use it to mark out your design, taking time to ensure the bowl of the spoon is spherical.

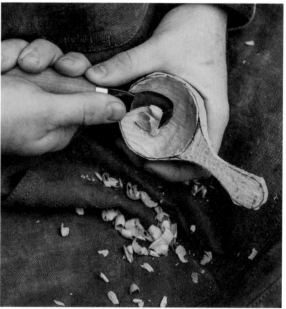

2 Clamp your piece of wood to a workbench or stable surface. Using a jigsaw with a curve cut blade, cut out the shape, being very careful since your piece of wood will be thicker than previous projects in this book due to the depth of the bowl of the scoop. You may need to work slowly to ensure a clean cut.

3 Once you have your blank cut out, start working on the bowl of the scoop with the hook knife. The scoop cut will work well to remove a good deal of waste material, and then the push cut can be used to refine the shape and make the bowl deeper.

4 Moving on to shaping the scoop, use the straight knife to start to remove stock material from the back of the bowl. You will be able to take off large amounts at once using the scissor cut. Remember to change the direction you are cutting by reversing the direction of the scoop in your hands. This will ensure you avoid cutting against the grain.

5 Take some time using the detail cut to create nice fluid transitions from the shoulders down to the end of the handle. Once you are happy with the shape of your handle, using the straight knife, revisit the bowl of the scoop to achieve an even thickness on the rim. You can shave small amounts off the top by keeping the blade very flat to the surface of the wood as you did when carving the cooking spoon (page 60).

6 When you are happy with the shape, you can begin sanding. Work up through the grits of sandpaper, starting at 120-grit moving through to 320-grit, until it is smooth to the touch and there are no obvious scratches from the coarser sandpaper.

7 Give the scoop a wipe down and a good coating of beeswax salve. Let this soak in overnight and then rub away any excess left on the surface the following morning.

6

CUTTING BOARD

Make a functional cutting board from reclaimed maple

Rough dimensions: 15¾ × 1¼ × 9¾ in (40 × 3 × 25cm)

A cutting board is essential in anyone's kitchen. This is a really simple and functional design that will introduce you to using the Shinto saw rasp and start you working on something that is larger in scale than a utensil. The board shown is a relatively large one, but you can make yours any size you want depending on the size of wood you are able to find.

Tools:
pencil
ruler
straight knife
clamp
Shinto saw rasp
sandpaper (see page 118)
cloth
beeswax salve (see page 122)

Wood:
maple

I used a slab of maple that I sourced from the offcuts pile at a local lumber supplier for this project. Maple is a great wood to use for a cutting board because it is so close grained. This means it is far easier to keep clean since there is little to no chance of food getting trapped in any open or raised wood grain. Its density and strength also means it will stand up to being regularly used to chop food. Other good alternative hardwoods I would recommend are sycamore, beech, and walnut.

1 The piece of maple I am using is an offcut from what would have been a large plank of timber. I am going to be using pretty much the whole piece and just rounding off the edges. You don't need to make a template for this, just mark a line in from the edge of the board as a guide for where you want the bevel to begin.

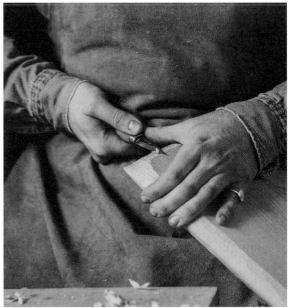

2 With the straight knife and using the pull cut, start to remove stock from the longest sides of the board. Make sure you switch between the two sides of the board to keep the bevel even.

3 Now start working the shorter ends of the cutting board using a combination of the pull cut and the push cut. As you are cutting across the grain, the use of the two different cuts is important in order to get a smooth and even finish.

4 Once you have removed a good deal of waste material and you are happy with the shape of the bevel, you can concentrate on shaping the corners. I have chosen to bring the corners to a point using the push cut. However, you could round them off depending on your preference.

5 Clamp the board to a workbench and start to use the saw rasp. The saw rasp cuts on the push stroke, so you can only use it in one direction, not back and forth like a conventional saw. It also has a coarse and a fine side. Start by shaping the edges using the coarse side and then when you are happy with the shape, you can use the fine side of the rasp to blend in any faceted edges.

6 The fine side of the rasp will give you a finish similar to using coarse sandpaper. When you start sanding, it is important to move up through the grits of sandpaper so that you are creating an even finish. Starting with a 120-grit and finishing on a 320-grit will give you a smooth, silky surface. It is worth taking some time with the rasp and sandpaper to achieve a quality finish.

7 Once the board has been sanded and wiped down, apply a very generous coating of beeswax salve and let it soak in overnight with the board propped on its end. Rub down and polish the surface the following day.

7

SERVING BOARD

Use reclaimed oak to carve a serving board

Rough dimensions: 14½ × ⅜ × 6 in (36 × 1 × 15cm)

Making a serving board is a good way to use the skills learned from spoon carving on a project that requires the use of new tools and techniques. Here, I show you how to utilize the shape of reclaimed timber to inform a design rather than trying to find the perfect piece of wood to fit a predetermined shape. More often than not, you end up with a more interesting board this way. It is a really nice way to work because it allows for shapes and curves to develop naturally and gives you the opportunity to let the grain and texture of the wood to take center stage.

Tools:
pencil
template (paper/cardstock)
jigsaw with curve cut blade
clamp
straight knife
drill
sandpaper (see page 118)
cloth
beeswax salve (see page 122)

Wood:
oak

You can often come across reclaimed oak in the form of old floorboards and discarded shelves, which tend to already be the perfect width and thickness to make serving boards from. The oak I use in this project is an offcut from a local cabinetmaker. Being able to source reclaimed lengths of timber in this form is ideal because no professional power tools or equipment are required. A jigsaw should be all that you need.

1 Mark out the shape of the serving board on the piece of wood with a pencil. Either create a template with thick paper or cardstock, using the dimensions above and the photo at left as a guide, or draw freehand, depending on the design you have in mind.

2 Clamp your piece of wood to a workbench or stable surface to ensure you make the cut safely. Cut out your design using a jigsaw, being careful around the tight corners. You will need to use a curve cut blade in your jigsaw in order to make a clean cut following your design.

3 Start by shaping the handle with the straight knife using the pull cut. Once you have rounded off the length of the handle you can use a push cut to shape the curve at the top. This is a good example of where you will encounter a change of direction in the grain. The best way to combat this is to keep pivoting your board so you are cutting from opposite directions.

4 Next, drill the hole in the handle. The size of the hole you want will depend on how big you decide to make your board. Choose the right size drill bit to ensure the hole is the correct size.

5 Once you have the hole drilled, you can use the very tip of your straight knife to tidy up and shape the edges.

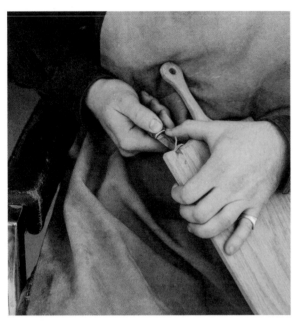 

6 After you have shaped the handle of the board, you can start to look at the shoulders. Here, a combination of the detail cut and push cut is useful to get a graceful sweep and to ensure that the transition from the handle to the shoulders is smooth.

7 You can soften and round off the sides of the board by working along each side following the grain. Using a pull cut again, you are aiming to refine the shape by removing nice thin, even, ribbon-like shavings, keeping your blade flat to the workpiece.

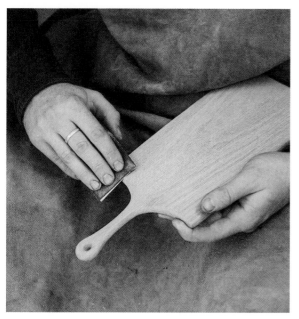 

8 Once you have shaped the board and are happy with the finish you have achieved with the straight knife, you can move on to sanding to even out the surface and give a lovely finish. Always working with the grain of the wood, start to sand and refine the edges moving up from 120-grit through to 320-grit.

9 Give the board a thorough wipe down with a cloth to make sure you have removed as much sawdust as possible. Use a clean rag to apply a coat of the beeswax salve, let it soak overnight, and wipe off any excess the following morning.

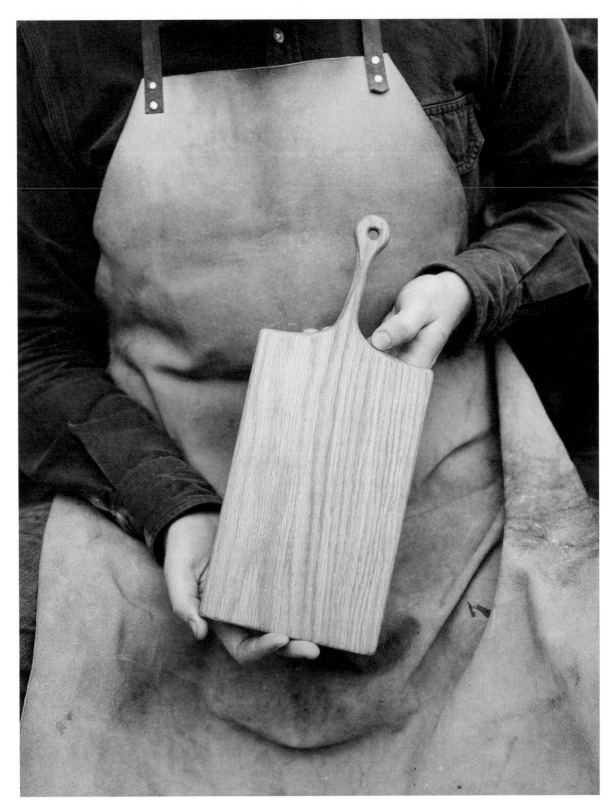

8

SMALL BOWL

Use green oak to carve a small bowl

Rough dimensions: 4 × 1¼ × 4 in (10 × 3 × 10cm)

This project is a great introduction to making vessels. I am a wood turner as well as a wood carver, so making bowls, pots, and vessels is something I'm really passionate about. Carving a bowl is, in principle, the same as turning one but the results are very different. Maybe it is the time that goes into it or the fact that you can see the effect every cut makes. This project will teach you how to use carving gouges, which are a great addition to your tool set.

Tools:
compass
pencil
clamp
10-mm carving gouge
6-mm carving gouge
jigsaw with curve cut blade
clamp
straight knife
hook knife
sandpaper (see page 118)
cloth
beeswax salve (see page 122)

Wood:
green oak

Oak is a fantastically versatile material. When it is green it is easily workable with hand tools, and when it dries it is immensely strong. I explain how to process green wood, but you can easily use dry offcuts or reclaimed lumber in its place. The reason I suggest using green wood is to make it easier when using the carving gouges, so if you can get ahold of a freshly cut branch you will find the work easier going.

1 Start by using a compass to mark out the diameter of your bowl. The size of your bowl will be determined by the size of your piece of wood. I am using a slab of green oak that I cut up from a log using a chainsaw, but splitting a smaller branch in two with an ax will work just as well.

2 Clamp the wood in place on a stable work surface and, using the 10-mm gouge, start to work across the grain from the near side of the bowl away from you. Make sure never to work toward yourself when using carving gouges. You may find it easier to stand up for this stage because it will allow you to put some weight behind your cut while keeping maximum control over the tool. Rather than trying to take as much waste away at once, focus on removing even curls with your gouge. This will be less tiring in the long run.

3 When you have reached the depth you are happy with you can begin to use the 6mm gouge to neaten up the edges and work right up to the perimeter line. You will need to start rotating the workpiece and to switch between the 10-mm gouge to remove the bulk of the waste and the 6-mm gouge to refine the inside of the bowl.

4 Once you have a smooth, even inside surface, you can use the jigsaw to cut the bowl out. Make sure that the blade of the jigsaw is long enough to cut through the thickness of the wood. You may need to go slowly to ensure a smooth cut.

5 Now start to carve the outside of the bowl with the straight knife. You need to use a variation of the pull cut using your thumb as an anchor point and cutting toward yourself with a clenching action. This cut will feel similar to the scoop cut when using your hook knife. Again, be very careful and remain aware of exactly where your fingers are, as you will be working in close proximity to the blade.

6 Once you have shaped the outside you can use the hook knife to even out the inside surface of the bowl and remove the chisel marks. The scoop cut and the push cut will work well here, but remember exactly where your fingers are positioned in relation to the knife to avoid possible injury. Sitting down and working close to your body will also help with stability and control.

7 Once you are happy with the depth of the bowl and the wall thickness (you can use a detail cut on the underside of the bowl to ensure that it is sitting flat on the bottom), take a moment to refine the rim of the bowl. Use the top of the straight knife blade to remove very small amounts of material. Let the bowl dry out for a few days before finishing. To aid the drying process you can wrap it in newspaper, but do not leave it near a direct heat source because this may cause it to split.

8 Once the bowl has dried out it will feel considerably lighter as the moisture content should have dropped. You can begin to sand the bowl, starting with the inside working with 120-grit sandpaper to even out the surface and remove any bumps quite quickly, then moving through the grits to achieve a smooth finish. The outside of the bowl can be sanded in exactly the same way.

9 Give the bowl a good wipe down with a cloth and apply a generous amount of the beeswax salve. Let it sink in overnight before buffing off the following morning.

Faceting

FACETING A COFFEE SCOOP

Although I finish most of my projects with sandpaper, sometimes I like to create a finish that just uses the knife blade. By making small, clean cuts that give a texture to the surface of the wood, you can create lots of individual planes that reflect the light and give a fantastic textured finish. You have to have a very sharp knife to do this, so it is a good idea to hone your blade before starting the finishing cuts. For further detail, see page 124 before embarking on this project.

Tools:
pencil
straight knife
sandpaper (see page 118)
cloth
beeswax salve (see page 122)

1 This project shows how to facet the back of a coffee scoop. This technique is really effective on this shape of spoon because there is a large surface area to work on. Start with a scoop that is already fashioned to its finished state apart from the back of the bowl (work through step 5 of the Coffee Scoop on page 76). Draw a horizontal line across the back of the bowl.

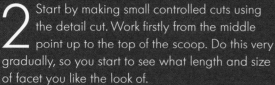

2 Start by making small controlled cuts using the detail cut. Work firstly from the middle point up to the top of the scoop. Do this very gradually, so you start to see what length and size of facet you like the look of.

3 Now begin working the other way, from the middle down toward the handle. This will ensure you get nice clean cuts without picking up the grain. Using the detail cut to take off small chips of wood, try to keep the depth and size of cut as consistent as possible. Remember this is going to be the surface finish, so you are aiming to keep the overall shape while still adding texture.

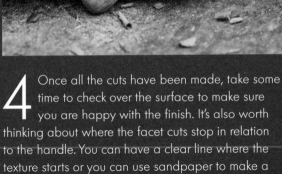

4 Once all the cuts have been made, take some time to check over the surface to make sure you are happy with the finish. It's also worth thinking about where the facet cuts stop in relation to the handle. You can have a clear line where the texture starts or you can use sandpaper to make a smooth transition.

5 When you are happy with the finish, give the workpiece a wipe with a cloth to remove any sawdust, and apply a coat of the beeswax salve. This will give the facets a real shine and reflect the light even more.

Scorching

SCORCHING A
COOKING SPOON

Scorching is a really effective and simple way to change the appearance and color of wood without losing the grain. It is a technique that works on many different types of wood, although I have found it to be most effective on hardwoods. In this project the handle of the walnut cooking spoon (see page 60) is scorched, which leaves it with a beautifully glossy, dark shine. Scorching only part of the spoon accentuates the graceful sweep of the shoulders as the handle transitions into the head. Although this is just one example of how to use this technique, I encourage you to experiment with applying it to other objects, be they spoons or boards, to create different finishes. You will need to make sure that you have a surface to work on that you do not mind getting a bit charred. A bit of old scaffolding board or plywood works well. It is also advisable to work in a well-ventilated area since you produce smoke when working with the blowtorch.

Tools:
blowtorch
protective gloves
protective goggles
cloths
sandpaper (see page 118)
beeswax salve (see page 122)

For this project you need a spoon where the head has been sanded to its final finish but the handle has only been roughly sanded and shaped using 120-grit sandpaper. This is because when you scorch the surface of the wood, the surface layer will burn and create a fine, almost charcoal-like layer. This is then sanded with a fine grit sandpaper to remove any excess.

―――

"Scorching only part of the spoon accentuates the graceful sweep of the shoulders as the handle transitions into the head."

―――

1 Hold the blowtorch in your dominant hand, and keep the end of the torch about 2 inches from the spoon. Work up and down the length of the handle, rotating the spoon with your free hand as you go to ensure an even distribution of charring.

2 Once you have scorched all of the desired area on the spoon and it has cooled down, give it a wipe down with a cloth and start to sand, working your way up through the different grits.

3 As you sand, wipe down the handle between each change of grit. You may need to rescorch areas after sanding and keep repeating the process until you have complete coverage.

4 Keep rubbing down the handle until nothing comes off onto the cloth. You can now apply a coat of the beeswax salve. It is best to use a different cloth to apply salve to the head of the spoon to prevent any of the scorched sawdust from the handle staining the unscorched wood.

Ebonizing

EBONIZING A
SMALL BOWL

The ebonizing process is one that is hard to believe even when you see it happening before your eyes. The basic principle is to create a chemical reaction between the natural tannins found in wood and iron oxide. Tannin is a tree's natural defense against predators and iron oxide is what we commonly know as rust. You can create an iron solution by steeping steel wool or iron nails in vinegar. Then by applying this to the surface of a wood that is high in tannin, such as oak, you can produce a chemical reaction that turns the wood black. Depending on the levels of tannin found in the wood, you will achieve different depths of black from blue and

purple hues to rich, jet blacks. In this project I show you how to ebonize a small bowl (see page 98). I advise using either oak or walnut for ebonizing due to the high tannin content in both woods.

Tools:
jar or container
water
white distilled vinegar
iron nails or steel wool
paintbrush
cloths

> *"The ebonizing process is one that is hard to believe even when you see it happening before your eyes."*

1 Fill a large jar or container with two parts water to one part white vinegar and add the nails or steel wool and leave. Within a week the liquid should start to turn an orange brown color as the iron starts to get rusty. Do not keep a lid on your jar because a small amount of gas will be produced as the vinegar reacts with the iron, which will need to escape.

2 Once the nails have been in the solution for at least a week, a layer of rust will form on the surface and the liquid will be brown or orange in color.

3 Using a paintbrush, start applying the rusty vinegar solution to the surface of the wood and allow the reaction to take place. If you are using oak, the reaction will happen immediately and you can see the color change in front of you. Observe how the color is developing and keep applying more solution if you wish to intensify it.

4 You can keep applying layers, allowing each layer time to dry, until the color does not get any darker. Once you are happy with the color, you can give the surface of the wood a wipe down with a cloth. This may result in some of the color rubbing off, but keep going until nothing more comes off on the cloth. You may want to leave the ebonized object somewhere to dry to allow the vinegar odor to evaporate.

5 When it is completely dry, apply a coat of the beeswax salve. You will need to use a clean cloth just in case any residual pigment comes off the object as you apply the salve. Let the salve sink in overnight and then rub down the following day.

SANDING

Sanding is a process that not every wood carver chooses to do. It is down to personal preference, and I have found that I prefer the finish and appearance that it gives. Every project in the book can be made with the sanding process left out. However, for me sanding gives the finished object that extra bit of refinement and produces something that has simplicity and elegance in its form. It also has practical applications. Sanding the bowl of an eating or cooking spoon produces a smooth surface that reduces the chance of food getting trapped and makes it easier to clean.

I use four different grades of sandpaper: 120-grit being the coarsest, moving up through 180-grit, 240-grit, to 320-grit, which is the finest. Working up through the different grits is really important—when you start with a coarse paper such as a 120-grit, it creates quite prominent scratch marks that you can see with the naked eye. As you then move up through the grits the scratch patterns become finer and finer, until you cannot see the scratch patterns on the surface without magnification.

One of the most important things to remember when sanding is always to sand with (in the direction of) the grain of the wood and never across it. If you sand across the grain you will find it very difficult to smooth the scratches out later. Sanding with the grain allows the grit on the paper to smooth the surface of the wood without tearing any of the fibers on the surface. When you use sandpaper, the surface of the paper will start to clog with a fine layer of wood dust. If you find this happens, wipe the sandpaper on a surface that the fine dust will cling on to, such as a leather or denim apron. You will find that sanding by hand does take time, but the finish you get will be well worth the time and effort you have put in.

> *"For me sanding gives the finished object that extra bit of refinement and produces something that has simplicity and elegance in its form."*

Beeswax salve

There are many different products on the market that you can use as a finish on wood, but I make and use my own beeswax salve to treat every piece of woodenware that I carve. It is a simple recipe that produces a gentle finish, which can be applied to the surface of wood to bring out the natural color and patina of the grain. As well as giving the product a protective coating against moisture, it is completely food-safe: everything treated with it is usable and washable.

This recipe will give you a large mason jar of salve, which should last you a good amount of time.

Tools and materials:
1 quart (1 liter) pure mineral oil
18 ounces (500g) pure beeswax pellets
large saucepan
heat source
mason jar
kitchen towel

1 Sterilize the mason jar using boiling water, or put it through a dishwasher cycle. Start by measuring out 18 ounces (500g) of beeswax pellets and 1 quart (1 liter) of mineral oil. The basic ratio is two parts mineral oil to one part beeswax.

2 Pour the oil into a large saucepan and set the heat to its lowest setting. Add the beeswax and heat gently until the pellets start to dissolve. Stir very gently to ensure the two ingredients have combined thoroughly. As soon as the mixture is clear, remove from the heat and set aside to cool.

3 Let the beeswax and oil cool for 5 to 10 minutes and then pour the mixture into the mason jar. Be careful in case the liquid is still hot.

4 Set aside and leave the lid open. Place a kitchen towel over the jar to ensure nothing drops in. Allow the salve to cure overnight and, once it is completely cool, it will set and turn cloudy. It is then ready to use.

5 Use a lid with a rubber gasket to seal the jar, and store in a cool, dark place.

TOOL CARE

Keeping your tools sharp and making sure they are well maintained is a really important part of a craftsman's practice. Dull or blunt tools can be dangerous, and it is always far safer to have a sharp blade to work with than a blunt one. A sharp blade is far more predictable and allows you greater control than a dull one. The less pressure and force you have to apply on the knife to make the cut the better.

I am going to explain how to sharpen both your straight knife and hook knife, and with a little practice you will soon notice the difference. Sharpening is something that can take a little while before you

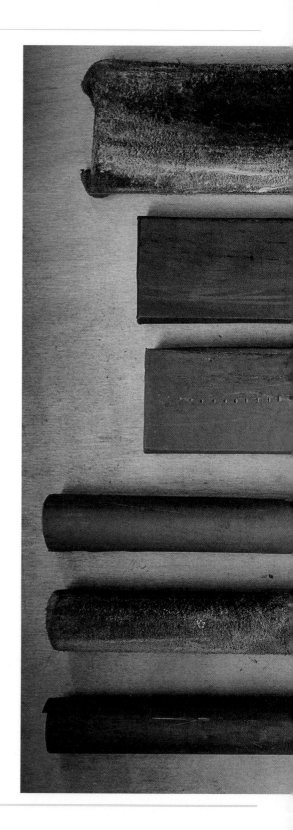

> ## *"Dull or blunt tools can be dangerous."*

become proficient, but once you have cracked it, you will be able to put a razor sharp finish on your tools every single time.

I learned very quickly to appreciate the value of having sharp tools. Carving becomes effortless and the control and detail in your work is far more sophisticated as a result. A good indicator of having successfully sharpened your blades is the sound a cut makes through wood. I liken it to the sound of fresh snow crunching underfoot. I have tried quite a few different ways of sharpening, from grinding wheels to sharpening systems, but I have come to the conclusion that sometimes the simplest really is the best.

Here I will show you how to create some basic tools to sharpen both your knives.

Straight knife

Tools and materials:
waterproof container
water
waterstone
Autosol (or alternative brand of metal polish)
leather strop (real leather)
cotton cloth

1 Fill your container with water and submerge the waterstone. Let it soak for 10–15 minutes—you will begin to see air bubbles escaping.

2 Once the waterstone has stopped releasing air bubbles, place it on a flat surface making sure the surface of the stone is still wet. You can splash a little on from the container if necessary. Make sure the coarse side of the stone is facing up, since this will be used first.

3 Place the bevel of the blade flat on the surface of the stone, holding the handle in one hand. Applying pressure on the blade with the other hand, keep the blade flat to the stone and push the blade away from you up the length of the stone.

4 Starting at the opposite end on the stone, place the other side of the knife bevel flat on the stone. Supporting it in the same way, pull the blade toward yourself down the length of the stone. If you are just refreshing the surface, you only need to make 10–15 passes on each side of the blade. Make sure you keep the surface of the stone wet throughout. If the blade is pitted (corroded), repeat this motion until you have a clean edge.

5 Now turn the stone over to the fine side and wet the surface to repeat the process. This is more of a honing process than a sharpening. Working on this side of the stone will polish the edge and remove the burr created when sharpening.

6 Finally, using a cloth, apply a small amount of the Autosol metal polish to the surface of the leather strop, or belt, and rub it in. Place the bevel of the blade flat on the surface at the bottom of the strop and pull the blade up toward yourself. Do this 10 times on each side of the blade.

7 When the surface has a shiny, polished finish, give the blade a wipe with a cloth. Be careful— the edge will now be razor sharp.

Hook knife

Tools and materials:
wet and dry sandpaper (600-grit and 1500-grit)
2 strips of soft leather
3 lengths of wood (12 inches [30cm] long ×
 2 inches [4.5cm] wide × ½ inch [1cm] deep)
PVA glue
3 lengths of dowel (9 inches [22cm] long ×
 ¾ inch [2cm] diameter)
marker pen
Autosol (or alternative brand of metal polish)
cotton cloth

1 Start by cutting one 10 × 5-inch (25 × 12cm) strip of the 600-grit wet and dry sandpaper, one 10 × 5-inch (25 × 12cm) strip of the 1500-grit wet and dry, and one 10 × 5-inch (25 × 12cm) strip of the soft leather. Now glue each of these strips to one of the lengths of wood, wrapping each strip right around the wood, making sure the seam finishes down the middle of one side. With the leather, make sure you have good contact and adhesion between the surface of the wood and the underside of the leather.

2 Repeat this first step and cut three more strips now measuring 5 × 4 inches (12 × 10cm) and glue each one around a length of dowel. These round sharpening tools you have made will allow you to get inside the curve of the hook knife.

3 Using the marker pen, color in the bevel of the blade. This will enable you to see where you have made contact with the sandpaper. If there is ink left on the blade you will know you have not made contact on that particular part.

4 Begin by sharpening the outside curve of the blade with the flat sharpening tools. Do each side of the blade separately. Start with the 600-grit and pull the flat tool across the bevel working from the top down toward the edge of the blade. Only work in this direction, never back and forth or you will dull the blade. Once you have removed all the ink from the bevel with the 600-grit paper, re-ink the bevel and repeat the process using the 1500-grit. You will notice the difference in the surface finish as it starts to become a lot shinier. Once you have completed this process of one side of the blade, switch and repeat on the other.

5 Now move on to the inside curve. Using the rounded 600-grit sanding bar, make a few strokes on the inside curve of the blade, keeping the surface of the paper as flat to the blade as possible. Move on to the 1500-grit sanding bar and repeat the process on both sides of the blade.

6 Now add a little of the Autosol metal polish to the surface of the flat leather strop and start to work across the outside bevel using the same motion as you did when sharpening. This will remove the fine burr that builds up during sharpening.

7 Repeat the same process with the leather strop on the dowel for the inside curve of the blade.

8 When the surface has a shiny, polished finish, give the blade a wipe with a cloth, being careful as the edge will now be razor sharp.

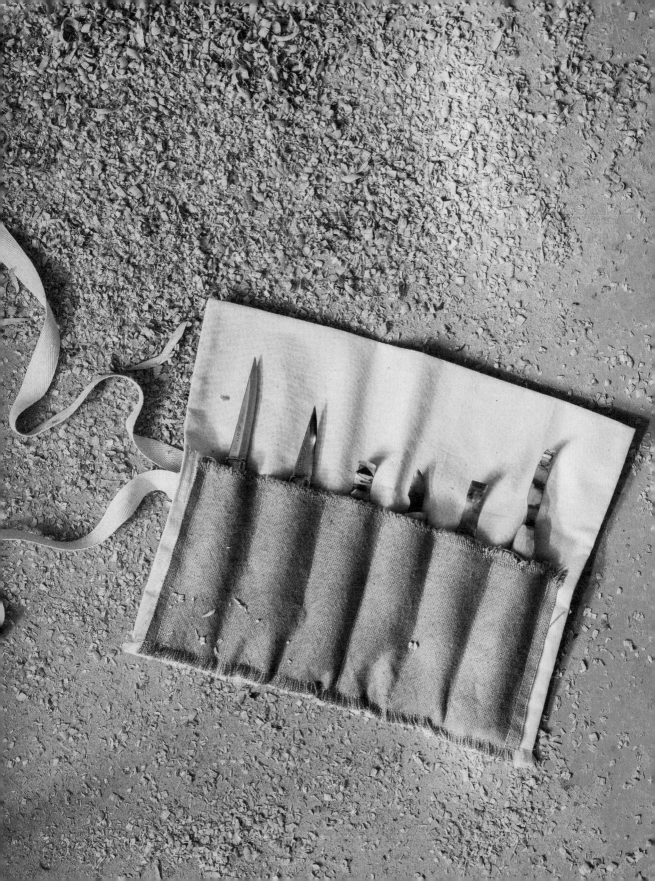

TOOL ROLL

Having spent all that time and effort sharpening your tools, it is important to store them safely to ensure they remain in good condition. Keeping tools protected means they will hold their edges for longer and require less sharpening over time. A tool roll is a really easy way of doing this and here I show you how to make a really simple one, which will give you somewhere to store your knives. I used a heavyweight canvas and a scrap of thick brown cotton fabric, but any material you have on hand will work. The heavier the weight of fabric the better, as this will give you more protection when folding over the fabric lip to cover the blades. I used a sewing machine to assemble the tool roll but if you do not have access to one, hand stitching will work just as well. The only difference will be the time it takes to put it together.

Tools and materials:
two pieces of heavyweight fabric (canvas, cotton, wool, denim, or leather all work well)
ruler
graphite pencil or chalk
sharp scissors
sewing machine
thread
pins
cotton twill tape

"Keeping tools protected means they will hold their edges for longer and require less sharpening over time."

1 Once you have all your materials laid out, mark out one rectangle measuring 15 × 22 inches (38 × 56cm) on your first fabric (A) and another rectangle measuring 13¼ × 6 inches (34 × 15cm) on your second fabric (B). Take a sharp pair of scissors and accurately cut along the lines until you have your two pieces of fabric to work with.

2 Fold the larger rectangle of fabric A in half lengthwise with right sides facing, and sew up the two opposite shorter sides. A simple running stitch on the sewing machine will work fine.

3 Turn fabric A inside out so that the raw seams are no longer visible. You can use the end of a pencil to push the corners gently out, giving you crisp, defined points.

4 Place the smaller rectangle of fabric B in line with the bottom, open edge of fabric A with right side facing up. Make sure it is centered and equidistant from both sides. Pin along the bottom roughly 1½ inches (4cm) from the edge. Sew through all three layers with a running stitch, attaching fabric B and sewing up the open edge of the canvas.

5 Now you can sew the two short sides of fabric B in position so it is completely attached to the canvas back.

6 Using your chalk or graphite pencil, divide the brown rectangle into six equal pockets and mark them with lines. Sew along each line,

"Once they are in, you can fold over the top of the canvas to protect the blades and roll."

making sure to reverse stitch at the beginning and end of every line to secure the thread.

7 Cut two 15¾-inch (40-cm) pieces of cotton twill tape and lay them out vertically on the back of the tool roll, facing opposite directions. Pin these in place.

8 Sew two parallel lines through each piece of tape to secure it in place. Make sure to remove the pins as you sew to avoid breaking your needle.

9 Your tool roll is now ready. Put your knives in the pockets and test that they fit. Once they are in, you can fold over the top of fabric A to protect the blades and roll it up. Wrap the ties around and fasten in a knot.

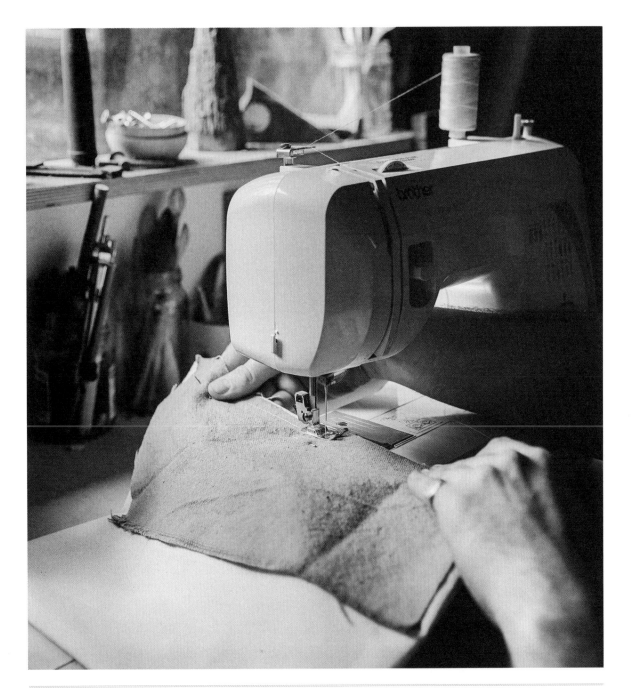

RESOURCES

All of the tools and materials used throughout this book can be found in local DIY stores and online, but here are a few other suppliers you can check out. My wish was to write a book that allowed people to get into carving without having to invest in expensive tools and set-up. It is always worth doing your research to see what is available to you locally. No matter where you are in the world, you should be able to access everything you need to begin.

AMAZON
www.amazon.com
Here you can source mineral oil, pure beeswax, Autosol metal polish, and a variety of other tools and supplies.

FOREST + FOUND
www.forest-and-found.com
I work full-time at my business, Forest + Found, in London, England, and happily respond to those who contact me for advice: contact@forest-and-found.com.

HOME DEPOT
www.homedepot.com
Sells lumber and supplies such as jigsaws, knife sets, and a wide variety of sandpaper.

SKIDMORE'S
www.skidmores.com
Family-run business out of Washington that sells woodfinishing creams and beeswax salves.

WOODCARVERS SUPPLY, INC.
www.woodcarverssupply.com
Sells a wide variety of woodcarving tools and supplies.

WOODCRAFT
www.woodcraft.com
Sells wood and wood carving supplies with an online catalog and stores in Pennsylvania, Maryland, and Virginia.

GLOSSARY

Autosol: a common brand of metal polish.

ax: a tool used for working greenwood.

bevel: the sloping surface or edge of a blade or cutting edge.

blank: the rough shape of a spoon or knife cut out of wood prior to carving.

bowl: the concave head of a spoon.

bulk waste: excess wood that needs to be removed before defining the shape of an object.

burr: the rough edge left on a blade after sharpening.

carving gouge: a chisel with a concave blade.

close-grained: when the fibers of wood are packed tightly together to form dense wood.

concave: a surface that curves inward.

curve cut blade: a specific jigsaw blade for cutting curves.

ebonizing: the process of using the chemical reaction between tannin and iron oxide to turn wood black.

faceting: a surface finish produced with the blade of a knife.

figuring: the distinctive patterning in wood grain.

finishing cut: the final cuts made with a knife before sanding.

forest services: the government departments in charge of woodlands.

grain direction: the direction in which the fibers are running through a piece of wood.

green wood: freshly cut wood with a high moisture content.

grit: the grade of sandpaper from coarse (120-grit) to fine (320-grit).

hardwood: dense wood suitable for carving, from broad-leaved trees.

heartwood: the dense inner part of a tree trunk that produces the hardest timber.

honing: the final stages of sharpening a blade; this removes any burr.

hook knife: a wood carving knife with a curved blade for hollowing.

iron oxide: the chemical compound made up of iron and oxygen that naturally occurs as rust.

knot: a tight whorl in the grain where a branch would have formed.

local authority: an administrative body such as a local council.

pure beeswax: beeswax without the addition of paraffin, used in most commercial polishing products, making it food-safe.

running stitch: a straight stitch, the most common used on a sewing machine.

saw rasp: a tool made up of double-edged saw blades.

scorching: the process of burning to create a blackened effect on wood.

shoulders: the transition between a handle and body of a utensil or board.

stock material: excess wood that has to be removed before defining the shape of an object.

storm-damaged: a tree that has been blown over or hit by lightning.

straight knife: a wood carving knife with a straight blade.

tannin: an organic acid present in trees as a natural defense system.

tree surgeon: A person who prunes or treats old or damaged trees.

waterstone: a sharpening stone that uses water as a lubricant.

wet and dry: a high grade of very fine sandpaper.

wood grain: the fibers running through the wood that form its pattern.

workpiece: The object being carved or worked on during a project.

INDEX

LAST WORDS

Carving is a craft that has been practiced for hundreds of years, creating both functional and beautiful objects throughout history, and it is my hope that we keep this heritage craft alive and keep on carving for hundreds of years to come.

I hope this book and the projects within it have given you the confidence and knowledge to go forward and work on your own designs, shapes, and forms.

Writing this book has been a journey. I have met some amazing and talented people along the way, and without them it would not have been possible.

I think I should start by thanking Judith Hannam from Kyle Books. When she first got in contact, asking if I would be interested in writing this book, my first reaction was, "What, me?" And I'm so glad she did as it has been a truly wonderful experience that has given me the confidence in my own work that I perhaps lacked, so I want to say thank you to her for having the confidence in my work to see the potential of it translating into book form.

I want to say a big thank you to Kyle Cathie of Kyle Books, who allowed this project to go ahead, and without her support and backing this would not have been possible. Sophie Allen, my editor, has been a massive part of the whole process; she has managed to decode my overly excited rambling emails, reigned in perhaps slightly over-ambitious and sometimes dangerous ideas, and has generally made the day-to-day of writing and constructing this book joyful.

There would, of course, be no book without the constant hard work and effort from Tina Smith, our amazing designer. From our very first conversation, I knew we were in safe hands, and she also has had to put up with my nonsensical ramblings on the phone and has managed to pull out the odd few words that did make sense and transform them into something that is beautifully clean and simple—thank you.

I had clear ideas in my mind of how I wanted the book to look and feel and this is where Dean and Jeska Hearne come in. They have made the book what it is. The constant effort, on their part, from the very first phonecall about working on this project, is humbling. Their vision for every single photograph has resulted in a truly beautiful book. They are two of the nicest, funniest human beings I have ever met, and I hope they will remain life-long friends.

I want to say thank you to Troo, Chris, Emma, and Adam from Tree Couture. Without their generosity and willingness to help I would not have been able to work with all the beautiful walnut and oak I have used for some of the projects in this book. It's fantastic to be able to work with such amazing craftsmen, and I hope to be able to do so for a long time to come.

My family have been the constant throughout this process. My brother, James, and Abi, for popping their heads around the workshop door checking in on me; my mum, Liz or Lis, as she is more affectionately known, offering words of wisdom and advice, not to mention love and support; to my Nana Jean Gray, who passed away in 2013, but one of the last things she said to me that has been a constant source of inspiration was, "Now you have built the workshop, Maxy, you can do anything," and so I am writing this book for her, of which I hope she would be proud.

This brings me to the last person I would like to thank, although there are not really the words to express my love and gratitude toward her— everything I do, everything I write, and everything I make would not be possible without the constant love, support, and a good measure of tolerance from my beautiful partner, Abigail, whom I love.

Thank you.